Different, Damaged,

Delivered

Chenel Banks

Copyright ©2015 Chenel Banks

All Rights Reserved. No part of this book may be reproduced or transmitted in any form or by any means, electronic or mechanical, including photocopying, recording, or by any information storage and retrieval system, without prior written permission from the author/publisher of this book, except for the inclusion of brief quotations in printed reviews.

Contents

Prayer…………………………………..…………….4

Dedication……………………………………5

Special Acknowledgements…………….6

Special Thanks……………………………7

Chapter 1: Different…Demons? Spirits?……..8

Chapter 2: Mind Games …………………...18

Chapter 3: Generational Curses……………33

Chapter 4: Deliverance……………………39

Chapter 5: Drop Your Baggage……………62

Prayer

Father God, I just THANK YOU for your mercy and your grace. I thank you for just being who you are. Lord, I thank you for just endowing me with your Ruach HaKadosh (breath) giving me life. I thank you for being Yahweh-Rapha (The Lord who Heals) as you continually heal every broken area in my life. I thank you for being Yahweh Yireh (The Lord will Provide) as you supply all of my needs daily.

Dedication

This book is dedicated to my children, Ta'Shayla Peaker and Duvowel Peaker Jr.

I love you both with my whole heart. Words cannot express the love I have for you. I have always tried to be the best parent and role model that I could be so that you know there are no limits when it comes to your goals and dreams. You two have always been my biggest cheerleaders. Just set your goals and DO IT!

Love,

Mom

Special Acknowledgement

First, I would like to give thanks to my creator, Yahweh, because without him, I am nothing!

To my parents, Richard (Butch) and Christine Banks, I love you so much. You have always supported everything I have done.

Andrea Freeman – Thank you for ALWAYS being in my corner encouraging me when I couldn't encourage myself. I Love You To Life!

Michelle Monk-Miller – Where do I start . . . I just want to thank you for mentoring and guiding me through this walk called ministry. I have learned so much from you: how to STUDY my bible, how to research and dig deeper, and I thank you for just for believing in me. You are an AWESOME woman of Yah!

Bridgette Banks-Hamilton – Thank you so much for always being there for me and never judging. We are more like sisters than cousins. No matter what I am going through, you encourage me through every situation and issue. I Love YOU to LIFE!

Erica Jones-Bullock – Thanks for always being there. You always come to the rescue. Love you, girl!

Special Thanks

Sueko Wesley, Monika Johnson, Monique Neely, Ron Green, Apostle Raymond Stansbury, Apostle Kevin Miller, Tonique Smothers, Nichole Williams, Shea Lemuel, Valencia Lee, Jeannine Edwards, Charone Prewitt, Stacey Smith-Davis, Catina McCall, and the entire Walking By Faith Ministries family.

Chapter 1

Different

Demons? Spirits?

I remember attending church with my aunts as a very young child and hearing the people of the church use this word, "deliverance." At that time, I had no idea what they were referring to or even what it meant. Often the church would hold deliverance services that would go into the wee hours of the morning, and if things got to be too much for the children, they would designate one of the older teens to take us younger children into another area to protect us from whatever spirits or demons they were casting out of someone.

Demons? Spirits? Being the inquisitive, observant child that I was (some might say nosy), I wanted to see what was happening, so I would sometimes tell a fib that I had to use the bathroom just so I could get a peek at what was REALLY happening in the sanctuary. What I would observe would be the pastor and several others praying for someone. They would be praying so intensely, speaking in tongues, and sometimes the person would fall out in the floor, and they would get on the floor, continuing to pray and pray. Sometimes I would hear them commanding something to leave the person.

Let's rewind a bit. As a young child, I was scared of everything. My parents and all of my family members always laugh and tell stories of how I was scared of EVERYTHING: the wind, the dark, dogs, clowns, baby dolls, costumes, people with glasses (and I wore glasses). At around the age of five or six, I was playing in my parents' bedroom. We lived an apartment, and in their bedroom, there was a door where the furnace was. Well, while I was playing, I saw something. What I saw was a scary looking creature, so scary I was paralyzed with fear. I couldn't move or scream. It looked at me and held its finger to its lips as if to gesture, "Shhhhh . . ." and then gave me a creepy smile.

Once I snapped out of it, I ran into the living room and told my dad. Of course, he came rushing to the room to see, and of course, there was nothing there. There were times I would see shadows of men in my closet at night and tell my parents. They would check and then let me sleep with them. I'm sure, in their mind, they probably thought I was a little "off" as the old folks would call it. I'm sure all my grandparents, aunts, uncles, and cousins thought I was weird.

Ok, back to the deliverance service. One service, in particular, the deliverance team was calling stuff out of a woman, and she was lying on the floor. They were praying over her, and that is when I saw it . . . something rose up out of her body, something that didn't look human, and I smelled a horrible smell, a smell I don't think I have ever smelled again. I ran back in the room with the other children and never told a soul . . . I was haunted by that image and smell for a very long time; I couldn't sleep. Now I know what all of those things that I saw and encountered were. They were spirits. Yes, I know it sounds crazy, but it is very real. See, when the enemy sent those spirits to me as a child, as he often does to children, it is desensitize them so they will think it's normal. These spirits will talk to children. They even have names. Parents often unknowingly refer to these things as "imaginary playmates" or "imaginary friends." They are not "friends" or "playmates." They are DEMONS!

Some people ignore the subject of demons completely. Others have a compulsive interest in them. You should not minimize the power of demon spirits in the world today, yet you must not become so preoccupied with them that you see a demon in everything that happens and in everyone around you. You should take a simple, literal, Biblical approach to the subject of demons. Do not study secular books about such powers of evil. Your only sources of study in these areas should be the Word of Yahweh or good, Christian literature.

Demons were originally like the other angels of Yahweh with the same attributes and positions as the good angels. When Satan rebelled against Yahweh, a portion of the angels participated in his rebellion. Yahweh cast them out of Heaven along with Satan. They were no longer good spiritual beings (angels). They became evil spiritual beings (demons).

"And there was war in heaven: Michael and his angels fought against the dragon (Satan); and the dragon fought and his angels.

And prevailed not; neither was their place found any more in Heaven.

And the great dragon was cast out, that old serpent, called the Devil, and Satan, which deceiveth the whole world: he was cast out into the earth, and his angels were cast out with him" (Revelation 12:7-9, KJV).

The enemy was already trying to take me out as a child. He knew before I knew the calling that I had on my life from Yahweh.

December 26, 2010, I had another encounter with a spirit. It was 5:33 a.m., and I was lying on my couch watching television at the time. I lived in an apartment, and all of a sudden, I heard someone running up the stairs in the building; then, immediately after, I was unable to move. I had that paralyzing feeling again that there was a presence in my house. I didn't see anything, but I clearly felt its presence. I felt the breeze of it go by me. I heard it in my bedroom going through my dresser drawers, but I could do nothing: I couldn't move, I couldn't scream, I couldn't even call out the name Yahshua. I was paralyzed with fear. It was like something was holding me down. But in my mind, I was screaming, Yahshua, Yahshua! Finally, I could sense its presence leaving because I felt the breeze come back by. I was thinking, please Lord help me make it leave. Then I felt like it was over the top of me, staring me in my face, as if to check to see if I was asleep. It was an extremely eerie feeling, and then it blew in my face, and I heard it run back down the apartment building steps. I jumped up and started SCREAMING at the top of my lungs. I was literally pulling my hair. Two of my neighbors ran over and were knocking on my door to check on me, asking if they should call 911. I couldn't even think of what to tell them. What was I supposed to say, "I just had a spirit in my house, and it held me down on my couch and was going through my dresser drawers in my room"? Not! They would have called the people with the white jackets instead of 911. I told them I would be ok and thanks for checking. So I'm quite sure they figured I had some sort of mental issues. I was so confused about what had just happened that I was embarrassed to tell anyone at first because if someone came and told me something that crazy, I probably would look at them with the side eye. But after that night, I REALLY knew and understood that demons and spirits are REAL.

The enemy was coming full force because he knew it was a matter of time before the ministry in me would be birthed.

Chapter 2

Mind Games

As we know, the enemy's primary playing field is in our mind. He knows that, if he can control our mind, he can control us. Remember in the last chapter; I stated that I was paralyzed with fear and couldn't move or even speak. That's what the enemy does. It's his number one goal to keep us stuck.

"For the weapons of our warfare are not of the flesh but have divine power to destroy strongholds" (2 Corinthians 10:4, ESV).

Satan wants to make your mind carnal (sinful, worldly, fleshly). Yahweh wants you to be spiritually minded. The greatest commandment includes loving Yahweh with all your mind. This is one of the main reasons Satan battles for your mind.

 "Jesus said unto him, 'Thou shalt love the Lord thy God with all thy heart, and with all thy soul, and with all thy MIND; This is the first and great commandment'" (Matthew 22:37-38, KJV).

Satan battles for your mind because it is closely tied spiritually to your heart and mouth:

"But those things which proceed out of the mouth come forth from the heart; and they defile the man. For out of the heart proceed evil thoughts" (Matthew 15:18-19, KJV).

Depression

To be depressed is to be downcast, sad, discouraged, or in low spirit. It includes feelings of despair, despondency, and dejection. Depression can lead to suicidal thoughts or actual suicide because of the hopeless feelings, which produce uncontrollable mental grief, sorrow, heartache, and crying. Sometimes Satan uses circumstances of life to lead to depression. For example, a great loss or fear of loss, suppressed anger, a low self-concept, unfulfilled expectations, and a negative attitude can all be used to cause depression. In Proverbs 24:10, we are warned about "fainting in the day of adversity" (troubled or distressed circumstances). Sometimes depression is caused by the negative attitudes of those around us through which Satan works. In Deuteronomy 1:28, Yahweh's people admitted, "our brethren have discouraged our hearts" (Spiritual Strategies, 12)

I was someone who battled with depression throughout my life for so many reasons. Failed relationships, low self-esteem, molestation (which I held on to until I was in my thirties at the hand of an older relative), fear of failing my children, fear of failing my parents. But I was able to cover these things up so well no one knew the real battle that was going on in my mind. It was like I would put on my "happy face mask" out in public, but once I was alone, the mask would come off, and the torment would start all over again. At one time, the enemy had me believing his LIES instead of Yahweh's grace and faithfulness. Yahweh could see me when I couldn't. His word stands true; he will never leave or forsake us. In my walk right now, I am struggling every day. The enemy never lets up; he wants to take me out; he throws all kinds of roadblocks to discourage me. Sending thoughts of loneliness, fear, and despair, he tries to isolate our every thought so we feel there is no way out of our situation, but we must use Yah's Word against these attacks.

"The thief comes only to steal and kill and destroy. I came that they may have life and have it abundantly" (John 10:10 ESV)

"Be strong and courageous. Do not fear or be in dread of them, for it is the LORD your God who goes with you. He will not leave you or forsake you" (Deuteronomy 31:6, ESV).

Scripture tells us that there is a battle going on in our minds. Our thoughts dictate our actions. That's why the enemy will do everything he can to get us thinking in the wrong direction. Sometimes, it's not our own thoughts that are holding us back; sometimes, it's that we've believed the negative things other people have spoken. Those words are like seeds. If you dwell on them long enough, they'll take root and become reality. There will always be people telling us what cannot be done, speaking negative things. Too often, we latch on to those negative words and develop what the scripture calls a "stronghold." That's a wrong thought or action that keeps us from Yahweh's best. The way you break those negative strongholds is by rejecting the lie and embracing the truth of Yahweh's Word. In other words, you have to choose to delete that negative file in your mind.

Fear is one the biggest strongholds or yokes that we encounter. A yoke is something that is put around the neck of an ox to help control the animal. It limits or restricts its movement. If the ox starts to get off course, the yoke is used to pull it back. Even though an ox is very powerful, this small yoke keeps it from doing what it wants to do. Some people don't realize today that they're living with a yoke around their neck. They wonder why they can't get ahead or why everything is a struggle. It's because of the yokes that are dragging them down. See the two different translations of Isaiah 10:27:

First, from the Amplified Bible, "And it shall be in that day that the burden of [the Assyrian] shall depart from your shoulders, and his yoke from your neck. The yoke shall be destroyed because of fatness [which prevents it from going around your neck]."

And second, from the English Standard Version, "And in that day his burden will depart from your shoulder, and his yoke from your neck; and the yoke will be broken because of the fat."

When fear enters, a seed is planted in the soil of your mind. However, WE determine whether or not that seed takes root and grows. Too often, we water the wrong seeds.

"But other seed fell into rich soil and produced grain; it sprouted, and grew, and yielded a crop— thirty, sixty, even a hundred times what was sown" (Mark 4:8, CJB).

"Leave no [such] room *or* foothold for the devil [give no opportunity to him]" (Ephesians 4:27, AMP).

So many people today are living with less than Yahweh's best because they've allowed fear to creep in and take root in their lives. Fear is the greatest weapon the enemy uses to try to hold us back. Fear is not from Yahweh. Scripture tells that fear brings torment. It's designed to paralyze us and keep us from Yahweh's blessings. Yahweh is greater than fear. His power in you is greater than any power that comes against you. But in order to walk in His power, you have to close the door on the enemy. See, the enemy can't have access to your life unless you open a door and give him access. That's why we have to be careful what we watch, what we listen to, what we read, and what we say. When we open ourselves to fear, we give the enemy opportunity.

Yahweh's desire is that we continually progress, that we reach higher heights and go to new levels. Oftentimes, as soon as we make the decision to step out in faith and obey Yahweh, the enemy brings in fear to try to stop us. He brings thoughts like, "What if you fail? What are other people going to think? You don't have what it takes." He does his best to use fear to try to convince us to shrink back and stay where we are. The Bible says that fear is a spirit. It plays on our emotions and holds us back. But the good news is that we have power over fear! The Bible says that perfect love casts out all fear. When we receive Yahweh's perfect love, we will have confidence about the future because we know His plans are for our good. I've heard it said that fear is an acronym for "false evidence appearing real." We must understand that fear is a lie.

"For God has not given us a spirit of fear and timidity, but of power, love, and self-discipline" (2 Timothy 1:7, NLT).

All of us will be tested in the area of trusting Yahweh with all things. But what's important to remember is that Yahweh's Word and presence and grace prevails over all circumstances. And we can see and know and feel His peace and power if we will simply trust and obey Him during experiences that we don't understand. Yahweh is:

- Our strong rock that cannot be shaken
- Our foundation
- Our hedge of protection
- Our deliverer
- Our justice
- Forever with us
- Everlasting

Yahweh endures with us, and we can trust Him with all things in all times, even when His purposes don't seem to make sense to us and we're not even sure how to apply His Word to our current circumstances.

Take your life back by taking your thoughts back. Don't allow the enemy to have access any longer. Instead, meditate on the Word of Yahweh daily and allow His truth to sink down deep into your spirit. Let His truth make you free.

Our minds work a lot like a computer. The way we program our thinking will determine how our lives are going to function. You can have the most expensive, powerful computer you can find, but if you load the wrong software, it's not going to perform at its best. In the same way, many people are not living a victorious life, not because there is something wrong with them, but because of what has been programmed into their thinking. They start believing the lies the enemy is programming in our minds. Just like a virus can slow down a perfectly good computer, our wrong thinking can keep us from our destiny. If you're going to live in victory, you've got to know how to hit the delete button. When those thoughts come to discourage you, HIT the DELETE button.

Take Aways

-

Chapter 3

Generational Curses

Generational curses, I know we have all heard this at one time or another within the church walls. First, let's try to define what this actually means:

A generational curse is basically a defilement that was passed down from one generation to another. A generational curse is a continual negative pattern of something being handed down from generation to generation. For example, suppose your mother, father, and/or grandparents were involved in witchcraft or were sexually immoral of some sort, and they have now given the enemy and his workers some ground in their life. If this was something that they were heavily involved in, they have opened the door for demons to enter. The Bible tells us that the sin of the parents can cause that same pollution to be handed down to their children.

"Our fathers sinned, and are no more; and we bear their iniquities" (Lamentations 5:7, ESV).

"Keeping steadfast love for thousands, forgiving iniquity and transgression and sin, but who will by no means clear the guilty, visiting the iniquity of the fathers on the children and the children's children, to the third and the fourth generation" (Exodus 34:7, ESV).

What sometimes happens is that not only is the uncleanliness handed down, but demons move right in and take advantage of this, often at a very young age in a person's life (often before birth). The person then goes through life struggling with the same bondages that their parents struggle with such as substance abuse, promiscuity, or mental illness. This goes way beyond learned behavior; children may learn to be messy if their parents are messy. This is a spiritual bondage that is passed down from one generation to another.

Generational curses are family illnesses that seem to just walk from one person down to the next (cancer is a common physical manifestation of a spiritual bondage), continual financial difficulties (they continually hit roadblocks in their finances), mental problems, persistent irrational fears, and depression. Once you've accepted Yahshua, those curses are broken, but often, the demons that entered in before you accepted Jesus still need to be cast out. In other words, the curse is already broken, and there's no need for you to break any generational curses. But the demons who entered into you through those curses before you accepted Yahshua may still need to be cast out. Demons don't leave on their own. If you have involved yourself in any sin or opened any doors in your life, then it's important that you clear up any legal grounds (or strongholds) that you gave the enemy in your own life relating to the bondage. Unforgiveness is a great way to "trigger" generational spirits, so I would be on the lookout for any bitterness or unforgiveness in your heart as well. Unforgiveness is a serious sin that blocks the forgiveness of your own sins (Matthew 6:15), which creates ample legal grounds for the enemy to come into your life. Unforgiveness in itself puts us into the enemy's hands (The Great Bible Study, 2003-2008).

Take Aways

Chapter 4

Deliverance

The Clean Up Process

In the first chapter, I mentioned "deliverance." Well, in this chapter, I will discuss exactly what deliverance is and its process.

What is deliverance?

Deliverance – The state of being saved from something dangerous or unpleasant, a rescue from bondage or danger, the action of being rescued or set free.

Deliverance is the expulsion of a bad spirit from a place, person or thing,

Deliverance is the destruction of any yokes or stronghold.

A yoke is something that ties two animals together, and the movement of one depends on the cooperation of the other. If one animal decides to be slow or sluggish, it means that the other one cannot move ahead. The yoke retards one's progress.

Deliverance is uprooting evil seeds planted by the enemy. The enemy is an expert in planting evil seeds in the life of a person.

"The Spirit of the Lord is upon me, because he hath anointed me to preach the gospel to the poor; he hath sent me to heal the broken hearted, to preach deliverance to the captives, and recovering of sight to the blind, to set at liberty them that are bruised" (Luke 4:18, KJV).

To understand what it fully means to be delivered or what deliverance is, we must comprehend a few very important facts and they are as follows:

What does it mean to be bound?

A person becomes bound by yielding to the weapons the devil uses to fight against them in spiritual warfare.

Bound – to confine, restrain, or restrict as if with bonds, to put under an obligation, to constrain with legal authority, to wrap around with something so as to enclose or cover, to fasten round about, to tie together, to cause to stick together, to take up and hold: combine with, to form a cohesive mass, to hamper free movement or natural action, to become hindered from free operation, to exert a restraining or compelling effect.

"For we wrestle not against flesh and blood, but against principalities, against powers, against the rulers of the darkness of this world, against spiritual wickedness in high places" (Ephesians 6:12 KJV).

The legal authority the devil has over man that enables him to hold us bound is called a PRINCIPALITY— a powerful ruler, or the rule of someone in authority. The word may refer to human rulers' demonic spirits, angels and demons in general, or any type of rule other than God Himself. It may also refer to the territory or jurisdiction of a prince: the country that gives title to a prince. The devil is the prince of the air.

The word *title* means *ownership, claim, right*. It comprises all the elements constituting legal ownership, a legally just cause of exclusive possession. When the devil develops a principality in our minds or our bodies, he produces what is called a stronghold. It is within our minds that the devil has bound us into thinking that this is the way a certain situation is supposed to be, and there is nothing that can be done about it. He convinces us to believe that something is real even though it is not. When we believe something in our minds, it not only alters the way we perceive a certain thing, but also how we begin to act and live according to what we believe. As you will recall, we said that the devil understands that gaining control of the mind is ultimately having control of the soul.

The devil, who is a deceiver, uses trickery to fight this battle of spiritual warfare, and because man is limited in his thinking, he often yields to the temptations of the devil, thus failing in the spiritual war. The devil understands that gaining control of the mind is ultimately having control of the soul. Contrary to popular belief, alcohol, depression, narcotics, are not what people are bound by; these are only the manifestations of the true bondage, and that is the mind. The Bible says

"For as he thinketh in his heart, so is he" (Proverbs 23:7). KJV)

The devil knows that the way a person thinks is how that person will act. If he can convince a person to believe something untrue, then he can cause them to fall and defeat them in this spiritual war. Therefore, the alcoholic thinks they need the alcohol in order to make it and are bound because the devil has control of the mind; the drug addict thinks they can't survive without it and are therefore bound by it because the devil has control of the mind. Deliverance cannot happen unless you first change the way you are thinking.

In 2000, I gave my life to the Lord and was baptized; I went to church every Sunday; I went to Bible study; I joined the Ushers Board and the Dance Ministry. In my mind, I had changed my life around. I am no longer who I used to be. Now, in my past, I was the kind of person who really didn't bother anybody unless you messed with me, and then I would go off. I didn't have that in-between place. I literally went from one to twenty-five and would see red, and it would take a lot to calm me down. I had a problem with anger and rage. However, I thought that because I was in church I no longer had an anger issue. Until one Sunday in 2004, when that anger appeared again, and I totally let it take me over. I went to someone's house and physically attacked them. Oh, I was so disappointed in myself and couldn't understand how this could have happened . . . HOW??? I'm saved . . . aren't I? The problem was that, when I got saved, no one explained to me that there was a process I needed to go through. No one told me that ALL my issues, all the junk, all the hurt and the mess, weren't going to miraculously disappear.

I needed to be delivered. I needed to learn how to pray, learn how to study my Word so that my sword would be readily available when the enemy would try to come and plant those toxic seeds in my mind. I was walking around naked with no armor, completely uncovered.

While deliverance can be a one-time event, it can also be a process. Sometimes it takes time to dig out all the junk in our souls and break down all those strongholds that we have probably carried for years. For deliverance to successfully take place, we MUST have an intimate relationship with Yahweh, which means a prayer life and renewing our minds every day according to the Word of Yahweh. When we don't have a relationship with Yahweh, we give the enemy fair game to come in and keep us stuck and to plant more of his bad soil in our minds.

Exodus 18:8-11, KJV tells us:

"And Moses told his father-in-law all that the LORD had done to Pharaoh and to the Egyptians for Israel's sake, all the hardship that had come upon them on the way, and how the LORD had delivered them. Then Jethro rejoiced for all the good which the LORD had done for Israel, whom He had delivered out of the hand of the Egyptians. And Jethro said, 'Blessed be the LORD, who has delivered you out of the hand of the Egyptians and out of the hand of Pharaoh, and who has delivered the people from under the hand of the Egyptians. Now I know that the LORD is greater than all the gods; for in the very thing in which they behaved proudly, He was above them.'"

When the children of Israel were set free from their slavery in Egypt, it was by Yahweh's sovereign intervention. They were snatched out of a place of oppression and sent to a place of great freedom. Through Moses, God proclaimed to His people that He was going to set them free, and then He did.

God's people were so overwhelmed in their hearts from the slavery and their suffering that they could not even believe freedom would ever happen. I have been in that dark place, and I'm sure you have, too. Sometimes we are so weighed down by our circumstances that we cannot imagine things will ever be any different. This is how the people of Israel were in their captivity. Their position of slavery was not just being in a state of servitude—the Egyptians feared them. The Bible says that the Egyptians saw that the Israelites grew in numbers the more they were oppressed. Sometimes the oppression you experience is because someone is afraid of you. So the Egyptians oppressed God's people fiercely. They intended to keep God's people under the tight fist of slavery forever.

God's people were taken out of slavery and released into freedom, and they went on their journey to their Promised Land, a land flowing with milk and honey. I want to tell you today that we, too, have a "Promised Land," but we have to be free to get to it! Remember that God's people had to walk through the Red Sea to get to safety. There is a walk we must take to get to freedom as well.

Free – not bound, confined, or detained by force, capable of moving or turning in any direction.

Deliverance is when God sovereignly reaches down and cuts the cords that bind us to our oppressors. Deliverance involves the hand of God severing the power of that thing over you. He supernaturally takes you from a place of oppression to a place of breakthrough by severing things in the spirit realm.

"I will love You, O LORD, my strength.
The LORD is my rock and my fortress and my deliverer;
My God, my strength, in whom I will trust;
My shield and the horn of my salvation, my stronghold.
I will call upon the LORD, who is worthy to be praised;
So shall I be saved from my enemies" (Psalm 18:1-3, ESV).

"And so, from the day we heard, we have not ceased to pray for you, asking that you may be filled with the knowledge of his will in all spiritual wisdom and understanding, so as to walk in a manner worthy of the Lord, fully pleasing to him, bearing fruit in every good work and increasing in the knowledge of God. May you be strengthened with all power, according to his glorious might, for all endurance and patience with joy, giving thanks to the Father, who has qualified you to share in the inheritance of the saints in light. He has delivered us from the domain of darkness and transferred us to the kingdom of his beloved Son, in whom we have redemption, the forgiveness of sins" (Colossians 1:9–14, ESV).

"When the righteous cry for help, the LORD hears and delivers them out of all their troubles. The LORD is near to the brokenhearted and saves the crushed in spirit" (Psalm 34:17-19, ESV).

It's a process to get to deliverance:

1. HONESTY

We have to be honest with ourselves first to recognize that we may need deliverance in a certain area or two! Any sin not confessed or repented gives the enemy or demons a LEGAL RIGHT to remain. So ask Yah to help you see yourself as he sees us, to illuminate anything that is not of him. As long as we hide or cover up things that are in us and make excuses, we cannot be set free.

"I acknowledged my sin to you,

and I did not cover my iniquity;

I said, 'I will confess my transgressions to the

LORD,' and you forgave the iniquity of my sin"

(Psalm 32:5, KJV).

2. HUMILITY

You are not proud or haughty, not arrogant or self-assertive. Humility requires complete trust in Yahweh, not our way, but Yahweh.

But he gives more grace. Therefore, it says, "God opposes the proud, but gives grace to the humble. Submit yourselves therefore to God. Resist the devil, and he will flee from you. Draw near to

God, and he will draw near to you. Cleanse your hands, you sinners, and purify your hearts, you double-minded. Be wretched and mourn and weep. Let your laughter be turned to mourning and your joy to gloom. Humble yourselves before the Lord, and he will exalt you" (James 4:6-10, ESV).

3. REPENTANCE

Repentance is turning away from anything that hinders your spiritual growth. And really meaning it. Repentance requires an open confession of all sin.

"Do two walk together, unless they have agreed to meet?" (Amos 3:3, ESV).

4. RENUNCIATION

Fall out of agreement with those dark things like sexual addictions, pornography, occult activity and reading your horoscope, and watching movies with occult themes. But renunciation requires action. It's making a clean break from these things, which may include an action like destroying anything attached to them. So if you repent from lust, you would destroy anything related to it. (All books, literature, games, movies, pictures, etc.)

"And many who had believed came confessing and telling their deeds. Also, many of those who had practiced magic brought their books together and burned them in the sight of all" (Acts 19:18-19 NKJV).

So, first you repent, and then you renounce those things.

5. FORGIVENESS

He expects us to forgive anyone who has wronged us.

"If we confess our sins, he is faithful and just to forgive us our sins and to cleanse us from all unrighteousness" (1 John 1:9, NKJV).

"For if you forgive others their trespasses, your heavenly Father will also forgive you, but if you do not forgive others their trespasses, neither will your Father forgive your trespasses" (Matthew 6:14-15, NKJV).

Forgiveness is a MUST it is essential for deliverance.

Forgiveness doesn't condone wrong behavior. It simply releases the person from the debt they owe you so that God can release you from the debt you owe from your own transgressions

6. PRAYER

This is your personal time with the LORD, when you are talking to him and he is talking to you.

"Be sober, be vigilant; because your adversary the devil walks about like a roaring lion, seeking whom he may devour. Resist him, steadfast in the faith, knowing that the same sufferings are experienced by your brotherhood in the world. But may the God of all grace, who called us to His eternal glory by Christ Jesus, after you have suffered a while, perfect, establish, strengthen, and settle you. To Him be the glory and the dominion forever and ever. Amen" (1 Peter 5:8-11, NKJV).

We must keep on the full armor of God at all times, stay in the word, kill our flesh, and have a continuous praise and prayer life. Praise silences the enemy. Praise is expressing to Yahweh thankfulness, adoration.

Take Aways

Chapter 5

Drop Your Baggage and Move Forward

Now that we have learned the proper steps to deliverance—even though it can be an ongoing process—now we can move out of our past and welcome in our future.

"Therefore, since we are surrounded by such a great cloud of witnesses, let us throw off everything that hinders and the sin that so easily entangles. And let us run with perseverance the race marked out for us, fixing our eyes on Jesus, the pioneer and perfecter of faith. For the joy set before him he endured the cross, scorning its shame, and sat down at the right hand of the throne of Yahweh. Consider him who endured such opposition from sinners, so that you will not grow weary and lose heart" (Hebrews 12:1-3, NIV).

The key words I want to point are *hinders* and *entangles*:

*Hinders – creates difficulties for (someone or something), resulting in delay or obstruction. To interfere with or set back.

*Entangles – involves (someone) in difficulties or complicated circumstances from which it is difficult to escape.

What's happened in your past is not nearly as important as what is in your future.

Where you're going is much more significant and important than where you've been. Some of us have been to some low places, and some of us are still stuck there. If you stay focused on the past, you'll get stuck there. We are dragging around all of this negative baggage from the past.

Somebody offended us last week, and we stuffed that in our resentment bag.

You lost your temper and said some things that you shouldn't have. Or fell into a backslidden state. Now that's in your guilt and condemnation bag.

Ten years ago things didn't work out in that relationship. And we still don't understand it. We put that hurt and pain in our disappointment bag.

We carry around our bag of regrets, all the things we wished we would have done differently.

This is the reason a lot of people don't have joy or enthusiasm for life: because we are weighed down with all this baggage which is not of Yahweh.

Yahweh doesn't want us to be resentful, hurt, or unforgiving. Take your life back by taking your thoughts back. Don't allow the enemy to have access any longer. Instead, meditate on the Word of Yahweh daily and allow His truth to sink down deep into your spirit. Let His truth make you free. Boldly declare His promises over your life: "The thief comes only to steal and kill and destroy. I came that they may have life and have it abundantly" (John 10:10, ESV).

"Let us not become weary in doing good, for at the proper time we will reap a harvest if we do not give up" (Galatians 6:9, NIV).

Yahweh did not create you to carry around all that baggage.

If the circumstances of life have taken away your joy, today is the day to get it back. You weren't meant to live this life feeling drained, depressed, and down. Yahweh wants you to be excited about your future and learn to enjoy each and every day. If you don't make the conscious effort to keep your joy, year after year you'll get more and more solemn. Not only will the enemy rob you of the joy that belongs to you, but he'll rob your family and friends of the gift that you have to give them. When you have joy, you can use that joy to influence the people around you for good. Joy is strength, and when you have joy, you can offer strength to the people Yahweh has placed in your life. Life is too short to live that way. At the start of the day, let go of the disappointments, the setbacks from yesterday. Start every morning fresh and new.

"Create in me a clean heart, O God, and renew a right spirit within me" (Psalm 51:10, ESV).

Don't let what somebody did or didn't do for you be an excuse for living with a sour attitude. Don't let a bad breakup, a divorce, a betrayal, or a bad childhood cause you to settle where you are.

Move forward and Yahweh will pay you back.

Move forward and Yahweh will vindicate you.

Move forward and you'll come to a new beginning.

Forgive those who hurt you . . . GET free from that stronghold. Forgiveness is not a sign of weakness but a sign of maturity.

Forgiveness doesn't condone wrong behavior. It simply releases the person from the debt they owe you so that Yahweh can release you from the debt you owe from your own transgressions.

When you make the choice to forgive and allow Yahweh to heal your heart, you will be able to receive His forgiveness for you, and you will walk in His abundant blessing all the days of your life! What is holding onto unforgiveness doing for you besides inviting its other counterparts—like bitterness, depression, and rejection—into your life? All of those things are toxic to your spirit. Holding on to things like unforgiveness, bitterness, depression, rejection is like carrying around a weight . . . the definition of a *weight* is *a heavy object to hold or press something down*. So every time we take on one of those characteristics, it's like we are collecting more and more weights. Anytime you are weighed down with something, it is restricting your movement just like the yoke I spoke about in earlier chapters.

The main person you are hurting by holding onto these things is YOU.

Nine out of ten times, the other person that may have hurt you is going on living their life. They have probably moved on . . . but not you because you are so hung up on keeping your unforgiveness because it's yours. When we choose these things over YAHWEH, we are basically telling him that we don't trust him or have faith in his Word. Imagine how he feels because he loves us so much. Now I'm not saying that this will happen overnight; it is a process. Don't you know that, when you forgive someone, that situation or person no longer has power over you!

"Remember not the former things, nor consider the things of old. Behold, I am doing a new thing; now it springs forth, do you not perceive it? I will make a way in the wilderness and rivers in the desert" (Isaiah 43:18-19, ESV).

"'The glory of this present house will be greater than the glory of the former house,' says the LORD Almighty. 'And in this place I will grant peace . . . '" (Haggai 2:9, NIV).

The scripture talks about how the glory of the latter day will be greater than the glory of the former day.

Today, get your hopes up! Enlarge your vision. Be expecting Yahweh to bring opportunities across your path.

When Yahweh sees you, He sees unlimited possibility. He sees unlimited potential. He sees unlimited resources. Yahweh's grace and favor in your life enables you to become what He sees. But first, you have to open your heart and take the limits off of your life.

We limit Yahweh in our thinking . . . Thoughts of doubt, unbelief, and unforgiveness in your heart will close the door to His favor. When you choose thoughts of faith and expectancy, you are opening the door for Yahweh to work in your life. You are taking the limits off. Put the weights down.

Nothing that has happened to you is a surprise to Yahweh.

The business that didn't make it, the relationship that didn't work out, did not stop Yahweh's plan for your life.

Now, the real question is this: Are you going to get stuck, fall into self-pity, become bitter, let the past poison your future?

Or, are you going to shake it off and move forward knowing that your best days are still up ahead?

"I do not consider myself yet to have taken hold of it. But one thing I do: Forget what is behind and strain toward what is ahead" (Philippians 3:13, NIV).

It's easy to go through life focused on what didn't work out, who hurt us, or the mistakes we've made.

As long as you're living in regret, focused on the negative things of the past, it's going to keep you from the bright future Yahweh has in store.

Yahweh has favor in your future that will supersede anything that you've seen! I don't know about you, but I want all my blessings and so should you.

You've got to let go of what didn't work out. Let go of the hurts and pain. Let go of your disappointments and failures.

You can't do anything about the past, but you can do something about right now. Whether it happened twenty years ago or twenty minutes ago, let it go and move forward.

If you keep bringing negative baggage from yesterday into today, it will poison your future. And we all know that poison is designed to kill you.

Yes, you may have had an unfair past, but you don't have to have an unfair future. You may have gotten off to a rough start in life, but don't use those things or, should I say, let those things use you, to condone holding on to stuff and keeping you stagnant.

It's not how you start that matters. It's how you finish. Prepare your heart and mind to receive the increase and expect to see greater things in your future!

Never hold on to anything tighter than you're holding on to Yahweh!

Take Aways

Authors Contact Page

For purchases please contact me at

Chenelbanks@yahoo.com

References

Hammond, F. (1973, 2010). Seven Steps to Deliverance. *Pigs in the Parlor* (pp. 41-44). Impact Christian Books.

Spiritual Strategies: A Manual For Spiritual Warfare. (n.d.). *Spiritual Strategies: A Manual For Spiritual Warfare*. Harvestime International Institute.

The Great Bible Study. (2003–2008). Retrieved from The Great Bible Study: http://www.greatbiblestudy.com/generational_curses.php

www.ingramcontent.com/pod-product-compliance
Lightning Source LLC
Chambersburg PA
CBHW060852050426
42453CB00008B/951